THE STORY OF
THOMAS JEFFERSON,
Prophet of Liberty

THE STORY OF

THOMAS JEFFERSON,
Prophet of Liberty

BY JOYCE MILTON

Illustrated by Tom La Padula

A YEARLING BOOK

ABOUT THIS BOOK

The events described in this book are true. They have been carefully researched and excerpted from authentic autobiographies, writings, and commentaries. No part of this biography has been fictionalized.

To learn more about Thomas Jefferson, ask your librarian to recommend other fine books you might read.

Published by
Dell Publishing
a division of
Bantam Doubleday Dell Publishing Group, Inc.
666 Fifth Avenue
New York, New York 10103

ISBN: 0-440-40265-4

Published by arrangement with Parachute Press, Inc.
Printed in the United States of America
February 1990

10 9 8 7 6 5 4 3 2 1

Contents

Introduction

Young Thomas Jefferson felt himself being lifted high in the air. The next thing he knew he was sitting on a pillow on top of a horse. The pillow bounced up and down with each step of the horse. It protected young Thomas from the worst jolts. Only the strong hands of one of the family's slaves kept him from falling to the ground.

The Jeffersons were leaving Shadwell, in the foothills of Virginia's Blue Ridge Mountains, and moving east to Tuckahoe, a plantation in the flat Tidewater country of coastal Virginia. Thomas was just two years old. When he was a grown man, he recalled this journey.

1

The year was 1745. In those days, Virginia was still an English colony. Shadwell, where Thomas had been born, was in the central part of Virginia, where adventuresome farmers had recently settled. To the west lay the Blue Ridge Mountains, mile after mile of tree-covered peaks, which only a few brave colonists had ever explored.

The eastern part of the colony, the Tidewater, was flat and green. English colonists had settled there more than a hundred years ago. The land was divided into large farms where slaves grew tobacco and other crops that were shipped back to England for sale.

The trip from Shadwell to the Tidewater country took several days. That was as long a journey as most Virginians ever took. Very few Virginians of that time ever saw England, the country they called "home." Most never even got as far as the northern colonies—Pennsylvania, New Jersey, and Massachusetts.

Boys from families like Tom's could expect to attend a one-room school if they were lucky. If they were very lucky they might also have a few years in college. The smartest of them might become country lawyers or even be elected to the Virginia House of Burgesses. But most would become gentleman farmers, who owned and managed large tobacco plantations. The actual work on the plantation was carried out by slaves, who were first brought to Virginia, against their will, in 1619.

When he grew up, Thomas Jefferson did become a farmer and a lawyer. He was also an elected representative. His mind was filled with ideas that took him far beyond the farms and wooded hills of Virginia.

At the age of thirty-three he wrote the Declaration of Independence, announcing the birth of the United States of America. He became ambassador to France, America's first secretary of state, vice-president, and the president of the United States. Along the way, he found time to become an inventor, architect, scientist, and philosopher.

Thomas Jefferson's ideas were not always popular in his own time, but they helped decide what kind of nation the United States would become. Today, more than two hundred years later, Thomas Jefferson's ideas are the backbone of American democracy.

Growing Up

Thomas Jefferson's father, Peter, was known to everyone in central Virginia. He was the local land surveyor, the expert who helped when farmers argued about the boundaries of their land.

His wife was Jane Randolph Jefferson. Her family was one of the first arrivals from England. Peter and Jane Jefferson already had two daughters when Thomas was born on April 13, 1743.

Peter Jefferson was best known for his strength. He was over six feet tall and broad shouldered. He was the strongest man in that part of the colony. One of Peter Jefferson's neighbors claimed he had seen him perform an amazing feat. Two large barrels filled with freshly picked tobacco were lying side by side on the ground. Each weighed about a thousand pounds. No other farmer in the country would even try to move one of these barrels without help. But Mr. Jefferson could handle both at once. Standing between the barrels, he grabbed their rims and tilted them upward with a mighty heave. A second later, both were sitting upright!

Many other stories were told about Peter Jefferson. Although he had only attended school for a few years, he was as clever as he was strong.

He loved nothing more than spending an evening reading in front of the fire. Even though he had little education, he read poetry, essays, and other books. His favorite author was William Shakespeare. His favorite saying was: "Never ask another to do for you what you can do for yourself."

Peter Jefferson had studied mathematics and surveying on his own, teaching himself from borrowed books. He became so skilled as a land surveyor that he was chosen along with a well-known professor to survey the boundary between western Virginia and North Carolina. A few years later, he was honored to draw the first official map of Virginia.

When Tom was only two years old, Mrs. Jefferson's cousin, William Randolph, died. Managing the Randolph plantation and raising the Randolph children now became the responsibility of Peter and Jane Jefferson.

Although they weren't far apart, traveling back and forth between the Randolph and Jefferson homes took a lot of time. Mr. Jefferson decided it would be easier for everyone if he moved his family to Tuckahoe, the Randolph farm. Tuckahoe was larger than the Jefferson home and could more comfortably fit the two families.

The Jefferson family made the trip east on horseback. Several wagons, carrying all their belongings, followed close behind. At Tuckahoe, they moved into one wing of the white frame farmhouse.

The Jeffersons owned 2,500 acres of land, but their own house at Shadwell was modest. Tuckahoe was more grand. Its rooms had high ceilings. They were filled with fine furniture and carpets. For Thomas, the most exciting thing

7

about Tuckahoe was a new playmate, a boy about his own age, also named Thomas— Thomas Randolph.

Tom was especially happy with his new playmate because he didn't have any brothers. He had three sisters; two older and one younger. Still another sister was born a few months later. Thomas Randolph also had sisters; two of them. That made eight children in all at Tuckahoe— and *six* girls! The two boys naturally made good friends.

The children all played together, chasing each other through the big rooms of the farmhouse, across the green lawns, and around the garden.

Three years after the Jeffersons had moved to Tuckahoe, when Thomas was five, Mr. Jefferson hired a tutor for all the Jefferson and Randolph children. There were so many children they had their own little one-room schoolhouse! Nearby there was a pond where the two boys swam when their lessons were over for the day.

Right from the beginning of his school days, Thomas was an outstanding student. According to a story later told in his family, he had learned to read even before his tutor arrived. Thomas probably picked up his love of books from his older sister Jane. Jane was Tom's favorite sister. Like Tom, she also loved music, and the two of them spent a lot of time together singing hymns and practicing the piano and violin.

The Jefferson family moved back to Shadwell from Tuckahoe when Thomas was nine years old. Not long after that, his father gave him his first gun. All young men in those days were expected to be good at hunting, and Peter Jefferson had high expectations for his son. He wanted the boy to be able to survive on his own in the woods. Thomas was told to take his gun out into the forest and not to come back until he had caught his dinner.

Thomas knew nothing about hunting. Still, he managed to corner a wild turkey. He chased it down and grabbed it with his bare hands. Then he took off the garter that held up one of his stockings, and he used it to tie the turkey to a tree. Once the turkey was pinned down, Thomas managed to take aim and shoot. Proudly, he slung the bird over his shoulder and carried it home.

Thomas had proved that he was tough

enough to survive in the woods. He soon learned to track possums and raccoons and to hunt foxes on horseback. But he never enjoyed hunting as much as many of his friends did. What he did like was meeting the visitors who stopped by to see Peter Jefferson. Shadwell was on the main road between the Blue Ridge Mountains in western Virginia and Williamsburg, the capital city in the east. Hunters, mountain men, and Indians all regularly stopped at Shadwell on their way to Williamsburg. Thomas never knew when he might come home to find a group of Indians camped out in one of the fields.

The visitor that impressed him most was King Ontassete, an important Cherokee chief. Ontassete was the leader of all the Cherokees in the region and a very dignified man. Peter Jefferson had met Ontassete during his travels west of the Blue Ridge Mountains, and when Ontassete and his followers camped at Shadwell, the chief of the Cherokees was invited for dinner.

A few years later, when he was still a teenager, Thomas happened to be in Williamsburg when Ontassete arrived with about two hundred followers. The chief had been invited to London to visit the king of England. Before he sailed, he gathered his group for a farewell ceremony. Since Tom had met Ontassete at Shadwell, he went to the Indians' camp to hear his parting speech.

There was a full moon that night, and when King Ontassete stood up he looked larger than life, with the moonlight glinting on his shiny black hair. He spoke in a deep, clear voice, and his gestures were bold. Thomas couldn't understand a word of Ontassete's speech, but he would never forget the king's dramatic appearance.

And he would never forget the way the king's people listened in silence, their attentive faces lit by the flickering flames of the campfire.

As soon as the Jeffersons had returned to Shadwell, Thomas was enrolled in a boarding school run by the Reverend William Douglas. Peter and Jane Jefferson wanted him to learn Greek, Latin, and French; the languages that he would need to enter college. Even though he loved Shadwell, Thomas was there now only during vacations and school holidays.

Like most schools in Virginia at that time, Dr.

Douglas's school had only one teacher—the minister himself. Ministers were some of the best-educated people in the colonies, but they did not make very much money. It was customary for them to earn extra income by teaching students and housing them with their own families.

Unfortunately, Dr. Douglas didn't know much about any of the languages he was supposed to be teaching. Maybe some of the students were fooled by Dr. Douglas, but Tom knew that this was not the best teacher for him.

Tom was not very happy at school, but his vacations at home lifted his spirits. Then, during the summer of 1757, when Tom was fourteen years old, Peter Jefferson fell ill. There were two doctors living near Shadwell. Jane Jefferson called in both of them, but neither one could do anything. Mr. Jefferson grew weaker every day. In August, he died.

In those days, there were many contagious diseases and few medicines to cure them. It was not unusual for people to suddenly fall ill and die. But it seemed impossible that this could happen to Peter Jefferson. In the eyes of his family and his community, he had been a giant.

13

Tom felt completely alone. "The whole care and direction of myself was thrown upon myself entirely," he remembered many years later.

Awful as it was, the death of Peter Jefferson did lead to one change for the better. Tom's mother moved him to a school near Shadwell so that he could come home on weekends. His new schoolmaster, Dr. Maury, was a much better teacher than Dr. Douglas. He had just four other pupils, and the five boys in the class soon became the best of friends.

One of the boys, Dabney Carr, owned a very fast horse. Dabney was constantly bragging about his horse and challenging the other boys to race against him. Tom's horse was slow and could never beat Dabney's in a race. Still, Tom got tired of listening to Dabney's big talk.

"We'll race the thirtieth of February," Tom is said to have told Dabney one day. "I promise you that on that day, your horse won't be able to beat mine."

Dabney may have had a good horse, but he was not the smartest boy in the class. He accepted the challenge. Then he began counting off the days until the race. February 26 . . . 27 . . .

28. . . . Too late, Dabney realized he had been tricked. There was no February 30!

Dabney laughed as hard as the other boys, even though the joke was on him. Tom was the class prankster, and everyone was fooled by him sooner or later.

Revolutionary Speeches

By the time he was a teenager, Tom had grown into a tall, thin boy with red hair. His face was covered with freckles, and his fair skin turned pink after a few hours in the sun. He was a better-than-average athlete, and he loved to dance, but somehow he never looked graceful. His hands and feet seemed too large for the rest of his body.

Tom spent three happy years with Dr. Maury. He attended classes in a log cabin in the Maurys' yard. The cabin was cramped, and in the winter it was sometimes chilly and uncomfortable. But Dr. Maury was an inspiring teacher, and by the time Tom was seventeen, he could read whole books in Greek and Latin. He was ready to enter the College of William and Mary.

William and Mary was a big change from the one-room log cabin in the Blue Ridge hills. It was an important center of learning in colonial America, and today it is the second oldest college in the United States. When Tom began there in 1760, it was already sixty-seven years old. The imposing college buildings were solid red brick. Nearly all the teachers had studied in England. The one hundred or so young men who studied there came from the richest families in the area. Some of them owned fine horses and carriages. Quite a few were not interested in going to class. Instead, they liked to dance, play cards, and enjoy the big-city life of Williamsburg.

But Tom worked hard, perhaps because he had less money than his school friends. It is said that he studied fifteen hours a day! To fit in all these hours of work, he stayed up until two o'clock in the morning, slept a few hours, and got up at dawn. He only took exercise breaks. There was a big rock about one mile beyond the town limits, and every day Tom ran to the rock and back home. Another sport he enjoyed was swimming. One friend remembered seeing him swim thirteen laps of a pond that was about a quarter of a mile across!

From time to time, Tom would get tired of doing so much work. Then, for a few weeks, he would hang around with friends who spent their days fox-hunting, playing cards, and betting on horses. When he was grown, Tom remembered these friends as "bad company." "I am astonished that I did not turn off with some of them and become as worthless to society as they were," he wrote many years later.

When he was tempted by this fun-loving crowd, Tom would ask himself what kind of reputation he wanted to have: "That of a horse jockey? A fox hunter?" Young as he was, he already knew that he wanted to be a lawyer—the best in Virginia if possible. Still, when Tom went home to Shadwell for summer vacation, he missed the dances and parties in Williamsburg.

Tom was now nineteen years old, and he was very interested in girls. When he was home for the summer, he wrote a good friend, curious to know how his friend's romance with a girl named Nancy was going. "How did Nancy look at you when you danced with her?" he asked. "Have you any glimmer of hope?"

Tom himself had a crush on sixteen-year-old Becca Burwell. He worried that he had missed a chance to see her at a wedding he did not attend. Later, when his vacation was over, Tom had a chance to dance with Becca. Face-to-face with the girl he liked, Tom was tongue-tied. It was all he could do to stammer out a few foolish sentences. He was shy about expressing his deeper feelings to a girl, even though he was clever when it came to talking in class or making jokes with his friends.

The most interesting friend Tom made during his college years was a fellow student named Patrick Henry. Tom and Patrick met at a friend's house the Christmas before they began their first year at William and Mary. From the first, everyone could see that Tom and Patrick were alike in many ways. Both came from the western part of the colony. Both played the violin. And both were great speakers. When Patrick Henry gave a speech, Tom would close his eyes and let his imagination be carried along on the "torrent of language."

Patrick Henry was a few years older than Tom. He was already a practicing lawyer, a member of the Virginia House of Burgesses, and the best speaker in Virginia.

The House was similar to a state legislature of today. Its members were elected by the people of Virginia to make laws. But since Virginia was really ruled by England, it had little real power. When the English Parliament passed a new tax, there was nothing the House could do but send letters of protest.

People in the American colonics resented having to pay taxes to England. It seemed to them that they got nothing in return. The money went to pay for England's wars. None of it was used for schools, roads, or other improvements in America.

It was not only the unfair taxes that angered the colonists. England also signed treaties with the Indians and the French which kept the colonists from claiming land on the frontier. The colonists could not speak for themselves in discussions that would influence their future. They were not even able to elect representatives to the English Parliament, so they had no say at all in the decisions that controlled their daily lives.

In 1765, the English Parliament passed the most unpopular tax yet. It was called the Stamp

Act. The colonists were ordered to buy stamps for legal documents, playing cards, almanacs, and newspapers—not just for letters! The money from the stamps helped pay for British troops that were stationed in America. In protest, the colonists chanted, "No taxation without representation!"

When Patrick Henry decided to make a speech about the new tax to the Virginia House, everyone knew that what he had to say would be worth hearing. Many spectators came to listen. They packed the lobby of the capitol building. Thomas made it a point to be there.

As often happened when Patrick Henry spoke, his speech caused an uproar. But later people argued about just what he had meant. What most people remembered was that at one point Henry started listing the names of famous rulers who had been murdered by people close to them.

"Caesar had his Brutus," he said, "and King Charles had his Cromwell."

Next, he mentioned the name of the current king of England. "And King George. . . ."

The members of the House got very excited. Brutus had killed Caesar. Cromwell had exe-

cuted King Charles. Was Patrick Henry trying to say that they should rise up against the king of England and kill him?

"Treason!" someone shouted. "Treason!"

But Patrick Henry just smiled. "And George the Third may profit by their example," he added. "If *this* be treason, make the most of it!"

Patrick Henry had not exactly called for a revolution. But he had given everyone something to think about: If the colonies' quarrels with England could not be settled, someday it might be necessary to fight for freedom.

Tom Jefferson was impressed. He later told a friend that it was Patrick Henry who started the "ball of revolution" rolling.

Monticello, the Little Mountain

In the late 1760s, while Patrick Henry was becoming one of Virginia's leading politicians, Thomas Jefferson was just beginning his career as a country lawyer.

Since no single town in western Virginia had enough clients to support a lawyer, Jefferson spent most of his time traveling. He rode from village to village on horseback or in a one-horse carriage. His companion on his travels was his slave, Jupiter. While Jefferson argued cases and wrote up legal papers, Jupiter handled the business of getting them from place to place.

Although Jefferson didn't have a lot of money, he was considered a wealthy man be-

25

cause he owned property. He had inherited his farmland, and the slaves who worked it, from his father. Jefferson wasn't about to give up his slaves. But he was uncomfortable about being a slave owner. He always called Jupiter his "servant."

Besides getting started as a lawyer, Jefferson was busy planning a new house to be built on land left to him by his father. The plot sat on the far side of the Rivanna River, across from Shadwell. A tree-covered hill, 857 feet high, made the land special. From the hilltop, Thomas Jefferson could see the breathtaking Blue Ridge Mountains. It was on this spot that he would build his future home, Monticello. In Italian, Monticello means "little mountain."

Building a house on top of a mountain, even a little one, was not easy. Before the work could begin, the builders had to cut down enough trees to build a road up the side of the mountain. What's more, Jefferson would not be satisfied with an ordinary house. He wanted his home to be made of bricks, not wood. The nails and bricks used to build Monticello were actually *made* there as it was being built!

Monticello was more than just a house. It was Jefferson's hobby. And his dream, too. In order to build it, he had to teach himself to be an architect. He ordered books on Italian and English architecture. He studied the books carefully, trying to figure out what made these fine houses so beautiful. He made hundreds of drawings. And, one by one, he solved all the problems that came up.

Like all plantation houses, the main house at Monticello was surrounded by outbuildings. These buildings housed the laundry, the slaves' quarters, the icehouse, and the stables. The kitchen was an outbuilding, too. One reason for this was that Virginians did not have screens for their windows or doors. Putting the kitchen outside the main house kept flies away from the rooms where the family lived. Jefferson wanted the outbuildings at Monticello to be made of brick, too. Monticello would be very different from other colonial houses.

Even the orchard would not be ordinary. Thomas collected specimens of exotic fruits from all over the world—nectarines, pomegranates, figs, quinces, and apricots. He asked advice from people who were experts at growing fruit. Soon he knew as much about orchards as anyone in Virginia.

The work on Monticello, begun in 1770, went slowly. In the meantime, the old Jefferson family house, Shadwell, burned down in a fire. Only one part of Monticello was finished; a square one-story outbuilding. Thomas lived there while he continued to plan and build his wonderful mansion.

When he was not planning his house, Thomas was visiting a young widow with whom he had become friends. Her name was Martha Wayles Skelton. She was small and slender, with thick auburn hair and hazel eyes. Martha's husband had died when she was just twenty years old.

Thomas and Martha shared a love of music. Thomas would play his violin while she accompanied him on the piano.

It is said that two young men who liked Martha once happened to arrive at her house at the same time. Standing in the entrance hall, they heard her and Thomas in the parlor, playing a duet. The two young men looked at each other and shook their heads. The music was so beautiful, they knew at once that the musicians must be in love.

Soon, Thomas and Martha got engaged. He ordered a mahogany piano from England as a wedding present for her. For himself, he ordered a supply of new stockings and a green silk umbrella. The wedding was held at Martha's home on New Year's Day, 1772. Martha was twenty-three years old and Thomas was twenty-eight.

Two weeks later, the bride and groom returned to Monticello, riding in a small carriage. When they started out in the morning, it was snowing lightly. But later in the day, a real storm whipped up. Some miles from the house, the weather got so bad, they had to abandon their carriage and ride horseback. Soon the horses were trudging through three feet of snow.

By the time they got to the top of the "little mountain" it was late at night. They were cold and hungry, and there was no one awake to welcome them. All the slaves had gone to bed. The house was freezing cold, and there was nothing to eat.

But the harsh circumstances of their arrival at Monticello didn't dampen their spirits. Thomas and Martha decided to drink a toast to their new life together. Thomas remembered leaving a bottle of wine behind some books in his library. The two of them started searching for it, pulling books off the shelves. Soon they were laughing so hard that the noise woke up the slaves.

For a few months, Thomas stayed at Monticello. He spent time with Martha and supervised work on the main house. But soon, troubles in the outside world called him away from the mountain.

Thomas had been elected to serve in the Virginia House in 1769. He had to go to Williamsburg to attend its sessions. Along with some of the younger members, he was part of a group that met to discuss political issues. Usually the conversation was about England's unfair treatment of the colonies. This group, known as the Committee of Correspondence, met at the Raleigh Tavern, near the capitol. Throughout the colonies, there were related committees, and they exchanged ideas by mail. Besides Thomas Jefferson, Patrick Henry was also an important member of this committee. And so was Thomas's old schoolmate Dabney Carr, the boy with the fast horse.

The Committee of Correspondence met in the early 1770s, but the quarrel between the American colonies and England was still deepening. The British Parliament had passed yet another set of taxes, including one on British tea. The colonists were forced to buy this tea.

In Boston, in the northern colony of Massachusetts, a group called the Sons of Liberty decided to stage a protest against the tea tax. One night, in the winter of 1773, the Sons of Liberty dressed up as Indians and sneaked onto a ship that was docked in the harbor. Before anyone could stop them, they had dumped many tons of tea overboard. This was called the Boston Tea Party.

Jefferson and the Virginia House sided with the Sons of Liberty. They even passed a resolution calling for a day of prayer in support of the protest. This made the British governor of Virginia very angry. He ordered the House shut down.

But many of the members refused to go home. They moved to the Raleigh Tavern and continued to hold meetings. By the time summer came, they had agreed with leaders from the other colonies to hold a meeting in Philadelphia to decide what to do next. This meeting was the First Continental Congress.

The Virginia delegation to the Congress included Patrick Henry, George Washington, and Jefferson's cousin, Peyton Randolph. Jefferson was only thirty-two years old, and he was not considered important enough to attend. He did, however, write an essay on his ideas about the problems with England. He sent one copy to Patrick Henry and one to Peyton Randolph, president of the Congress. Peyton Randolph showed the essay to many people.

In his essay, Jefferson had written that Parliament had no right to pass laws for Americans. He also said that the king ought to be a servant to the people, not the other way around.

Some people thought these were dangerous ideas. But many people, in Europe and in the American colonies, were beginning to think this way. The members of the First Continental Congress wanted England to treat the colonies more fairly. They thought they would eventually settle their differences with Parliament and King George. They did not want to overthrow the king. To them, Tom Jefferson seemed like a young hothead, whose grand philosophy would not solve the immediate problems of taxation. It was sometime later that these members of Congress began to realize that the problems with England could not be easily solved, and that the colonies might need to rise up and declare their independence.

All Men Are
Created Equal

Today, we remember Thomas Jefferson as the author of the Declaration of Independence. But he almost did not get a chance to be part of the Congress where this historic document was written.

In 1775, when the Virginia House elected its delegates to the Second Continental Congress, Jefferson was passed over again in favor of three more well-known leaders: George Washington, Peyton Randolph, and Patrick Henry. At the last minute, however, the Virginians decided to elect an alternate. They picked Thomas Jefferson. He would go to Philadelphia if one of the regular delegates couldn't serve.

The Congress opened in May 1775. About six weeks later, Peyton Randolph was called back to Williamsburg. Thomas was asked to replace him. He left for Philadelphia immediately.

At first, Thomas did not make much of an impression. He seemed shy and not interested in the work of the Congress. He was constantly reading and tinkering. The hot Philadelphia summer turned his curiosity to scientific experiments on weather conditions.

But in the evenings, when the delegates got together to talk over their work, Jefferson did a lot of talking. The other delegates were impressed. They saw that he had a talent for putting ideas into words.

While the delegates to the Congress argued about how best to solve their problems with England, the people of Massachusetts were already fighting against British soldiers.

In April of 1775, the British army commander in Boston heard a rumor that the Sons of Liberty, the famous leaders of the Boston Tea Party, had stored some guns outside Boston. He sent soldiers to investigate. The soldiers got as far as the village of Lexington, where they found the village square filled with armed farmers. A British officer warned the men to put down their guns, but the farmers stood their ground.

Suddenly, the sound of a rifle shot rang out.

No one was ever quite sure which side fired that first shot of the Revolution, but the news spread quickly. From the surrounding villages, men grabbed their guns and went out after the British soldiers. More shots were exchanged in the village of Concord, but the farmers managed to chase the soldiers all the way back to Boston. The battles of Lexington and Concord were the first of the Revolution. Eight patriots who loved America died in these battles. Because the American Revolution inspired other people living under tyranny to rebel, a famous poet wrote that the first shot of the Revolution was "the shot heard round the world."

With the blasts of gunfire still in its ears, the Second Continental Congress organized an army of soldiers from all of the colonies to help the New Englanders, or patriots. George Washington was elected commander in chief of the Continental Army. The Revolution was under way.

But what were the Americans fighting for? Did they want to be completely independent of the British? Did they want to remain dependent but fight a war to settle some of their differences—like those over taxation? Many people had different opinions about the Revolution. They argued about the problems with England and the best way to solve them. Not everyone wanted to fight a war.

Some members of the Congress thought it would still be possible to settle their differences with the king. The British army was one of the best in the world. It was hard to imagine that the colonists could win the war. Some of the delegates were not sure they wanted to be independent. Cutting the colonies' ties to England was a big step.

A whole year went by.

The break with Britain was not sudden. The Boston Tea Party in 1773 and the colonists' refusal to pay the stamp tax in 1765 were two early signs of trouble between the colonies and England. When the Second Continental Congress met, colonists had already died in battle. Everyone knew that the colonies would probably declare independence from England. But the

Congress still needed to send an official document to Britain—a declaration—which would state that the colonists were going to separate from the mother country. This document also had to convince the people of America and Europe that this big step was necessary.

A committee of five men was chosen to write the statement that the Congress would send to England. This statement would be known as the Declaration of Independence. Benjamin Franklin was a member of the committee. So was John Adams of Massachusetts. The other men chosen were Roger Sherman, Robert Livingstone, and Thomas Jefferson.

Many years later, John Adams told how he and Thomas Jefferson argued over who would do the actual writing. In the beginning, said Adams, Jefferson wanted him to have the honor. But Adams insisted that Jefferson should write it.

In the end, Jefferson agreed to write the Declaration. He shut himself up in his room. He used a special folding desk that he had designed himself. It was so small he could hold it on his lap.

He worked until late into the night, day after

day. He wrote by hand with a quill pen: "We hold these truths to be self-evident, that all men are created equal. . . ."

Everyone has certain rights, Thomas went on, "to life, liberty, and the pursuit of happiness." No government could take these away.

The Declaration of Independence was filled with new ideas about how government should work. It said that government existed to serve the people. If the government failed to do its job, then the people had the right to overthrow it.

Jefferson worked on the Declaration for about three weeks. When it was finished, the committee sent it on to the Congress. For three days the delegates argued. They picked apart every word and phrase Jefferson had used. Listening to all these distinguished men criticize his work made Jefferson very nervous. Benjamin Franklin tried to cheer Jefferson up by telling him funny stories.

In the end, the Congress made very few changes in the Declaration. This was partly thanks to John Adams. He defended every word Thomas had written.

On July 4, 1776, Congress voted to approve the Declaration of Independence. This is the

day we celebrate as Independence Day every year. All the delegates knew that they were making a decision that would change their lives—and change the course of history, too.

A Narrow Escape

Thomas Jefferson's important work in the Congress was over. In September he returned home. While George Washington and the Continental Army continued to fight the British, Jefferson helped to run Virginia. His homeland was not an English colony anymore. It was a state. In November 1777, after approving the Declaration, the colonies became states in the newly formed nation, the United States of America.

At that time, there were many cruel laws in Virginia. A person could be hanged for stealing. There were even laws against witches. Jefferson helped to rewrite the laws to make them more humane.

Jefferson had many ideas for improving Virginia's education system. One bill that he wrote called for a system of public schools. Poor children, both boys and girls, would get three years of free schooling—and more, if they were outstanding students. Another of his bills called for building a public library.

Most of these bills did not get passed into law. Many of them, especially one that proposed to end slavery, were too advanced for the time. The other Virginia assemblymen were willing to fight a war to be free from English rule, but they were not ready to change all the laws that governed them. They agreed that public schools for poor children were a good idea, but claimed they were too expensive. As for getting rid of slavery, they ruled this out as completely impractical.

Thomas Jefferson owned slaves himself, but he still felt that slavery was immoral. "Nothing is more certainly written in the book of fate than that these people ought to be free," he once wrote.

He called slavery a "cancer" that threatened to

kill the young democracy. He had seen that the Indians and the settlers could not seem to live together in peace. As more settlers came to live in the east, the Indians were forced to move farther and farther west.

Jefferson suggested that freed slaves could settle in the west, too, if the government would set aside land on the frontier.

The assembly voted down this idea. It seemed too radical—and far too expensive, they said. Nobody wanted to give up his slaves.

Jefferson was wise to be so concerned with slavery. It was a growing problem that would cause America to fight the Civil War in 1860.

Of course, no one asked the slaves what they wanted. But it was a good guess that many of them would not have been eager to leave Virginia to live in the wilderness.

Although many of the bills that Jefferson fought for did not become law, some did. The one he was most proud of guaranteed freedom of religion.

Before the Revolution, the Church of England had been the official church of the land. Everyone had to pay taxes to support it. Thomas wanted church and state to be separate. Citizens of Virginia could belong to any church they chose—or to no church at all.

In the United States today, everyone can follow the religion of his or her choice. But in Jefferson's time, it was a controversial idea. Some Virginians called Jefferson's bill the work of the devil. Nevertheless, the Assembly eventually passed the bill by one vote.

Thomas Jefferson had made a name for himself with all the work he was doing to shape the new government while the Revolution continued to rage. In 1779, he was elected governor of Virginia. This was an important job.

Meanwhile, to the north, the patriots were still fighting the British army. In 1776, the British had captured New York. They chased George Washington and his troops all the way to Valley Forge, in Pennsylvania. Washington fought back. In 1777, there were big battles in New Jersey.

Washington's army was short on guns and ammunition. Many of the soldiers did not even have shoes. They had to wrap their feet in rags to keep from getting frostbite. Many times, they did not have anything to eat.

Year after year, the war dragged on. Fighting in the south began in Georgia in 1778 and spread to South Carolina, and to North Carolina in 1780. But so far, Virginia had been lucky. Virginia volunteers were fighting with the patriot army, but there had been no fighting in the state itself. Thomas's main job as governor was to persuade the Assembly to send soldiers, guns, and supplies to help the patriots in the other colonies.

By 1780, the British had begun to lose the war. France had decided to send help to the Americans. But the British were not quite ready to admit defeat. They had a secret plan—a surprise attack on Virginia.

On December 31, 1780, Thomas Jefferson was walking in the garden of the governor's mansion in Richmond, where he and his young family were living, when an American officer appeared on horseback. The officer had alarming news. British warships had been sighted off the coast. The enemy was on its way!

The people of the Tidewater country watched helplessly as the stately British warships sailed into Chesapeake Bay and up the James River. They were even more frightened and angry when they learned that the invaders were led by Benedict Arnold, an American general who was fighting on the British side.

Jefferson called for soldiers to defend the state. But there was not much more he could do. Virginia's best troops had already been sent to help the patriots in the Carolinas. A few days later the British marched into Richmond.

Jefferson had escaped across the river. From there, he watched helplessly as Benedict Arnold's troops paraded through the streets of the capital.

A small force of Americans hurried south to fight the invaders. Its leader was a dashing young French officer, the Marquis de Lafayette. Lafayette had left a life of luxury in France to help the Americans fight. He was full of enthusiasm for the ideals of liberty that the colonists were fighting for.

Jefferson had only met Lafayette a few times. But he had liked the young Frenchman right away. Unfortunately, Lafayette's little army was not strong enough to drive the enemy out of Virginia. More British troops arrived from North Carolina in May of 1781. The members of the Virginia Assembly retreated all the way west to Charlottesville, the town nearest to Monticello.

Jefferson had already sent Martha and his three young daughters back home to Monticello. Now it was time to join them. He wished Lafayette luck and rode off to Monticello.

A few days later, an American captain named Jack Jouett stopped in a roadside inn called the Cuckoo Tavern. There he learned that a group of British soldiers called Tarleton's Raiders was on its way to make a surprise raid on Charlottesville.

Jouett leaped into the saddle. British raiders were already on the main road. But he knew a shortcut. He raced forty miles along backwoods trails to reach Monticello and warn the governor.

Thomas Jefferson was having breakfast with his family and some members of the Assembly. When the guests heard Captain Jouett's news, they hurried to Charlottesville to warn the rest of the Assembly. Jefferson immediately sent his wife and daughters off in a carriage to safety.

He stayed behind until almost the very last minute. Then he mounted his favorite horse,

Caractacus, and rode away from his beloved home. There was nothing more for Jefferson to do. It was up to the army now to stay and fight the British.

Before Jefferson got very far, he learned that the British soldiers were already coming up the main road. The only escape was along a trail that led over the mountain. Near the top of the mountain, Jefferson stopped at a spot where there was a good view of the countryside. He took out his telescope and studied the scene below. He could actually see the British soldiers riding in the streets of Charlottesville.

This battle, called Tarleton's Raid, had been embarrassing for Virginia's leaders. Like Jefferson, the members of the House of Delegates had fled Charlottesville, all the way to the western side of the Blue Ridge Mountains. Some people accused the governor of being a coward. The Assembly passed a resolution calling for an investigation of his conduct.

The Assembly's investigation found that Jefferson had done nothing wrong. But he was hurt that his fellow Virginians tried to blame him for what happened, and he stepped down as governor.

In October of 1781, the main American army, led by George Washington, arrived in Virginia. The Americans defeated the British at Yorktown, Virginia. This great American victory was the final defeat for the British—and the end of the American Revolution.

Already shaken by his political setback, Jefferson faced real tragedy in 1782. His wife, Martha, died on September 6. Thomas Jefferson was thirty-nine years old. Of the six children that had been born to him and Martha, only three were still alive—Martha, whom everyone called "Patsy," Maria, nicknamed "Polly," and the youngest, little Lucy Elizabeth, who died soon thereafter.

Overcome with sadness, Jefferson locked himself in his room. He refused to eat. The only person he would let near him was his oldest daughter, ten-year-old Patsy.

After three weeks, Jefferson ordered a servant to saddle his horse. He spent the next few days riding. At dawn, he would get on his horse, and he wouldn't come home until it was dark. Finally, Jefferson was ready to put his sorrow behind him. But he never married again.

The Jeffersons Go
to Paris

On July 5, 1784, Thomas Jefferson and his daughter Patsy stood on the deck of the sailing ship *Ceres* and waved good-bye to America. Thomas had been asked to represent the United States in Europe. Polly, who was only six years old, was left behind in the care of an aunt.

Now eleven years old, Patsy was very excited. She was thrilled to be crossing the ocean, especially on a brand-new ship like the *Ceres*.

At the end of the twenty-one-day passage, Patsy wrote to tell her sister Polly that France was "the most beautiful country . . . a perfect garden."

France was a nation with a long history and

respected culture. The newly formed United States did not have a constitution yet. It did not even have a president. But there was important business that could not wait. Before the war, American farmers had sold their crops to England. Who would buy them now? Congress wanted to trade with all the nations of Europe, especially France. To do that, the United States needed to sign treaties that would state the rules of trade.

During the war, Congress had sent Benjamin Franklin to represent America in Paris. But by now Ben Franklin was seventy-eight years old. A few months after Jefferson's arrival, Ben Franklin decided to return to Philadelphia. John Adams became the American ambassador to England. Thomas Jefferson took over for Benjamin Franklin in Paris.

Representing the United States in Paris was a very important job. Jefferson was honored to be chosen. And he was happy to be far away from Monticello and its sad memories.

But the job was not going to be easy. Benjamin Franklin had been very popular. He had a casual and friendly manner. He wore plain clothes and homemade eyeglasses, and he had a funny story for every occasion. The French thought he was the typical American, not impressed by wealth or royalty. His experiments with electricity were famous all over Europe.

Even though Thomas Jefferson had written the Declaration of Independence, many French leaders had never heard of him. At first, he had a hard time getting the French to like him. But little by little, he managed to make friends.

Patsy also had a lot of changes to get used to. Soon after she and her father arrived in Paris, she was enrolled in a convent school. Her classes were taught by nuns. Her schoolmates were all girls. They lived at the convent all week long and went home only on weekends.

Patsy was amazed to find that three of her classmates were royal princesses. They wore a special blue ribbon draped over one shoulder, so no one would forget their royal status.

At first Patsy wondered if she would ever feel comfortable in her new school. She didn't know much French. Often she could hardly understand what her teachers and the other girls were saying.

Patsy was tall and thin, with red hair. Like her father, she had lots of freckles. The other girls nicknamed her "Jeffy." They helped her with her French lessons, and soon, she could even tell jokes in French! Before long, she started to like her school, and she felt right at home in Paris.

Patsy's father, however, never felt at home in Paris. He missed his younger daughter, Polly, who was now eight years old. After being in Paris for two years, with his treaty work still not done, he decided to send for her.

Polly joined Patsy at her convent school. But she, like her father, was always a little homesick for Virginia.

Jefferson's work in France went beyond writing treaties. It was his job to study everything possible about life in France and Europe—especially scientific life. By writing reports home and sending recent inventions, agricultural products, plant and animal specimens, books, and art, he helped his young nation keep pace with Europe. Jefferson especially liked this part of his job.

One of the new inventions that Jefferson sent home to America was a portable printing press. Wooden matches with phosphorus tips were another. Jefferson did not have matches at Monticello. He had used cumbersome flints to light fires. He thought it was a great treat to have matches handy on the table beside his bed, so that he could light his oil lamp in the middle of the night without getting up.

One of the scientists Jefferson met was a man named Buffon. Buffon was an expert in the plants and animals of the world. But he had written a book saying that the animals in America were smaller than the animals in Europe!

Jefferson knew this was wrong. To prove it, he asked a friend in America to send him the skin and skeleton of a moose. He then had the skin stuffed so that Buffon could see what an American moose looked like. The stuffed moose turned out to be seven feet tall. When Buffon saw it, he admitted that he had made a big mistake!

Jefferson even studied French cooking. Everyone in Paris was talking about an exotic new dish called macaroni. Jefferson bought cases of macaroni to ship back to Monticello. He also bought a machine for making pasta. He arranged for James Hemings, the slave who came with him to Paris, to study to be a French chef. Later, Jefferson and Hemings made a deal. As soon as he had taught another of Jefferson's slaves to cook, Hemings would become a free man.

While Jefferson was in France, leaders from all over America were gathered in Philadelphia to write the Constitution for the new country, which was adopted in 1789. When he heard what was in the Constitution he was pleased. He liked how it arranged the new government with a president, senators, representatives, and judges. Even so, he thought there was something missing—a Bill of Rights—which would list personal freedoms that could not be taken away by government.

Jefferson wrote to his friends at home about his idea. His advice meant a lot to them. They agreed with him, and in 1791, the Bill of Rights was added to the Constitution. It made eight amendments, or changes, to the Constitution. It promised the government would not interfere with the people's basic freedoms, like freedom of religion and freedom of speech.

Because he was stationed in France, Jefferson could not actually help write the Constitution or the Bill of Rights. But he did have the chance to witness another great historical event: the start of the French Revolution.

The French king, Louis XVI, and his queen, Marie Antoinette, were not popular. Jefferson's friend Lafayette, the French officer he had met in Virginia, was now living in France again. He was one of the leaders of a group that had been inspired by the American Revolution. They hoped to give the people of France more say in how the government was run.

To Lafayette and his friends, the author of the Declaration of Independence was a hero. They told Jefferson their ideas and asked for his advice.

On June 11, 1789, Lafayette stood up at a meeting of the French Assembly and suggested that the members should vote on a declaration of rights for France. Lafayette held up a paper and read in a ringing voice. "Nature has created men free and equal."

Many of the phrases in Lafayette's declaration sounded a lot like the Declaration of Independence. Jefferson was glad to see that his ideas about human rights and self-government were being debated in France. And he hoped that they would be accepted peacefully. He soon realized that it was not going to work out that way.

The weekend after Lafayette's speech, the streets of Paris were filled with people. Some carried muskets; others carried pistols or swords. Some were waving farm tools.

Jefferson was visiting the home of a friend that day when someone rushed in with dramatic news. The crowd had stormed the Bastille, the prison where King Louis locked up his critics, and set the prisoners free.

Many wealthy Parisians were scared. They wanted the people to have some voice in making the laws, but now they feared the revolution was getting out of hand. Some people were calling for the arrest of the king of France himself!

This was an interesting time in France. But Jefferson's work there was nearly done. Patsy was seventeen years old and finished with school. It was logical that she should marry soon. Though Jefferson worried that an American man might be less well educated than his daughter, he did not want Patsy to stay in France. He thought it would be better for both of his daughters to return home.

Packing for the return home was a tremendous job. The Jefferson family's luggage for the trip filled thirty-eight boxes and hampers. And this was just the beginning. Jefferson later sent home seventy-eight more crates. Among the belongings were six cast-iron stoves, a harpsichord, and 145 rolls of wallpaper. There were paintings, too, and silverware, and mahogany tables and chairs.

But the most precious belongings were Jefferson's books. "I cannot live without books," Jefferson said once. When he was in Paris, Jefferson had visited the bookstores every single day. Later, one of the most important libraries, the Library of Congress, purchased Jefferson's collection.

Three months after the Jeffersons returned home, Patsy married her cousin, Thomas Mann Randolph. Marriage between cousins was common at that time. Thomas Randolph was the son of the only other boy at Tuckahoe, where many years before young Thomas Jefferson had been otherwise surrounded by girls.

He was a good man, but he was young and inexperienced at farming. He and Patsy relied on her father for help and advice. Later, Jefferson helped them buy a farm near Monticello.

Jefferson had planned to return to France sometime after Patsy's wedding. But he never did get the chance. A week after the wedding, President George Washington asked Jefferson to take the job of secretary of state. Jefferson accepted and moved to New York City, the temporary capital of the United States.

Much of what Jefferson saw and heard in New York made him unhappy. In France, he thought, revolution had gone too far and become too violent. The king and queen had been killed and their heads had been put on poles and paraded through the streets. But America, Jefferson thought, had the opposite problem. Perhaps the Revolution hadn't gone far enough in changing people's ideas about government.

Many officials were now worried that the government would go too far in the direction of equality. Many of the rich and powerful thought that they deserved to run the government. They doubted that a majority of men, many not well educated, could choose a good leader.

The organization of government and the roles of citizens and elected officials were hotly debated. In 1790, *democracy* was almost a bad word. Even Thomas Jefferson was careful about using it.

Jefferson and his chief rival in the government, Alexander Hamilton, were on opposite sides of this debate. Hamilton, who was secretary of the treasury, wanted the federal government to have a lot of power over the people. Jefferson worried that making the government strong would interfere with the people's freedom.

Jefferson's supporters claimed that Hamilton secretly wanted America to be ruled by a king again. Hamilton's supporters said Jefferson was a wild-eyed revolutionary.

The feud between Jefferson and Hamilton led to the creation of America's first political parties. Those who agreed with Hamilton were called Federalists. Federalists favored a strong national government. Businessmen and people who lived in the cities were more likely to be Federalists.

Members of Jefferson's party were called Republicans. (The party was not the same as the Republican party of today.) The Jefferson Republicans did not want a strong federal government. Their ideas favored farmers (including rich plantation owners) over businessmen.

The argument between the two parties makes today's politics look tame. Republican newspapers made fun of John Adams, who was a Federalist, calling him "Toothless Adams." Federalist newspapers claimed that Jefferson was an enemy of God because he believed in freedom of religion.

John Adams and Thomas Jefferson had worked together on the Declaration of Independence but were now political rivals with very different beliefs. In 1796, Jefferson ran for president. John Adams was his opponent. At the time, political parties didn't run candidates for vice-president. John Adams won the election. And since Jefferson was runner-up, he became vice-president.

President
Thomas Jefferson

In 1800, Jefferson again ran for president against John Adams. This time he won, but by only a few votes.

Even before Thomas Jefferson was declared the winner of the election, his supporters were singing a victory song. It was called "Jefferson and Liberty," and the words went like this:

> From Georgia up to Lake Champlain,
> From seas to Mississippi's shore,
> Ye sons of freedom loud proclaim,
> The reign of terror is no more!

What reign of terror were Jefferson's admirers talking about? The administration of President John Adams!

Today, it would be hard to imagine politicians from one political party accusing the other of a "reign of terror."

But not in 1800. The Federalists disliked the Jefferson Republicans. Some Federalists thought that Jefferson only wanted to be president so he could "stop the wheels of government."

Jefferson himself called the election a second revolution. He and his supporters were not even sure that the Federalists would let them take office, even though they had won the election.

President Adams did everything he could to make life difficult for Jefferson. At the last minute, he named many new judges—all Federalists—who would be sure to oppose the policies of the new president.

On the night before the inauguration, President Adams rode out of town at two o'clock in the morning. This hurt Jefferson's feelings. He and John Adams had once been friends. Mrs. Adams had taken care of Polly when she arrived in England, on her way to Paris. Now the second president and the third president could not talk to each other.

After the inauguration Jefferson moved into the White House. The president's home was still unfinished. Some rooms still had no plaster on the walls and no wood on the floors. But President Jefferson didn't really need the space. He lived alone in the big house with only his secretary, Captain Meriwether Lewis.

Sometimes Jefferson was lonely.

He worried about his daughter, Polly. She had married her cousin, John Eppes, when Jefferson was vice-president. Now, she was expecting her second baby. Like her mother, Polly was often ill. She stayed in bed through most of her pregnancy. Jefferson wrote her encouraging letters. He teased her that having a baby was no worse than "a knock on the elbow." But in his heart, he was very concerned about her health.

After the baby was born, Polly was weak. Slaves carried her on a stretcher to Monticello from her home four miles away. Jefferson hurried home from Washington.

He tried everything he could think of to

make Polly get better. He planned special meals. He suggested different kinds of medicine. But none of his ideas worked. Two weeks later, Polly died.

After Polly's death, Jefferson was closer to Patsy and her children. When his grandchildren came to visit, he would spend hours playing with them. Some people thought it was undignified for the president to spend so much time playing. Jefferson, now about sixty, paid no attention to the complaints.

Thomas Jefferson was a hardworking president. He spent ten to twelve hours a day at his desk and wrote all his own speeches and letters. Even George Washington had help writing his letters.

All his life Jefferson had worked for equality for all people, regardless of what they thought or how much money they had. As president, he continued to be a fair man.

While John Adams was president, the Federalists had passed laws that allowed them to put Republican newspaper editors in jail. When Jefferson was elected, he could have used the same laws to silence the Federalists. He was angry with

the newspapers that complained about him. But he still believed that people had a right to talk and write as they pleased. He decided to ignore the attacks and trust the good sense of the people.

Before Jefferson took office, the Federalists had predicted that he would ruin the country. They believed that the nation would fall if Jefferson's ideas of liberty and equality were put into practice. How could the Congress write laws if there were so many voices to hear? But Jefferson believed that a nation grows strong when it listens to many opinions. The Americans of his day strongly agreed, and they reelected him president in 1804. Still, some Federalists could not give up the idea that Jefferson's ideas would cause trouble. They complained that the president was "wild for equality."

What had Jefferson done that was so wild?

In addition to his ideas about government, perhaps it was Jefferson's behavior that his opponents did not like. Washington and Adams had been very dignified men. Both of them liked to dress up. Some people even called Washington "Your Highness." But Jefferson did not care for fancy clothes. He wore plain shoes without buckles. His stockings were wool, instead of silk. He did not bother to powder his hair or wear wigs, as other gentlemen did. He spoke simply and was not a great speechmaker.

Jefferson also disliked customs that put one person above another. At dinner parties, it was the custom to ask the most important people to sit next to the president. But when Jefferson gave a party, he let his guests sit wherever they wanted to sit. His tables were round, so no one sat at the head of the table. And he liked to have visitors drop in whenever they felt like it, without an invitation.

Sometimes groups came from faraway states to meet the president. On his first New Year's Day in office, Jefferson met some farmers from Massachusetts. The farmers presented him with a New Year's gift—a cheese made from the milk of four hundred cows. The cheese was four feet across, and it weighed 1,235 pounds!

New Year's Day was a big holiday in Jefferson's time. But his favorite holiday was the Fourth of July. Every year on the Fourth he had a party to celebrate the country's birthday—the day it declared independence from England. On this day, anyone could come to the White House and shake the president's hand.

When Thomas Jefferson became president in 1801, the western boundary of the United States stood at the Mississippi River. The land beyond, once claimed by Spain, had been turned over to France. This land had never been colonized by Europeans, so the Indians lived there undisturbed. Very few Americans had ever been west of the Mississippi.

Thomas Jefferson now had an opportunity to buy this huge area, called the Louisiana Territory, which stretched from the Mississippi River all the way to the Rocky Mountains, and from Canada in the north to the Gulf of Mexico in the south.

How did Jefferson get this opportunity? By 1802, after the chaotic years of the revolution, France had a new leader named Napoleon Bonaparte. He was a soldier who wanted to establish France's glory by overpowering the other nations of Europe. The United States did not want France for a neighbor, and Napoleon needed money to pay for his wars. In 1803 France sold the Louisiana Territory to the United States for about fifteen million dollars. Suddenly the United States was twice as big!

No one knew much about the new territory. Jefferson asked his secretary, Meriwether Lewis, to lead an expedition into the unexplored land. Lewis and a friend, Captain William Clark, picked forty-three men to go with them. In May of 1804, they started up the Missouri River from St. Louis.

While they were gone, Jefferson had a clerk collect whatever reports about the territory he could find. Some were tall tales. One said that somewhere in the territory there was a mountain of salt 130 miles high!

Jefferson's enemies laughed at this report. Did the new land also have a lake of molasses? they asked. How about a valley of pudding?

But the fantastic story about the salt mountain only showed how little was known about the Louisiana Territory and how wise Jefferson was to send Lewis and Clark on their trip of exploration. By getting to know the people, the land, and the animal and plant life on the far side of the Mississippi, Jefferson blazed a trail that would be traveled by many men and women in the 1800s who wanted a better life. Purchasing the Louisiana Territory was one of Jefferson's greatest achievements.

In 1804, the same year that Lewis and Clark left St. Louis, the Republican and Federalist feud came to a strange end. Alexander Hamilton had discovered that some of his fellow Federalists in New York and New England wanted to withdraw from the United States. These Federalists worried that the recent Louisiana Purchase would make the northeast less important to the government. Aaron Burr was Jefferson's vice-president. He agreed to help with the Federalist plan, even though he served a Republican president. Alexander Hamilton told people about Burr's secret part in the plan. Aaron Burr became very angry. He challenged Alexander Hamilton to a duel.

Early one morning, the two men met in Weehawken, New Jersey, near the banks of the Hudson River. They turned their backs to each other and walked in opposite directions for several yards. Quickly they turned and fired their pistols. Burr shot to kill. Hamilton died the next day.

Dueling was against the law, but it was an old European practice. Aaron Burr escaped by running away.

Soon Jefferson began to hear strange rumors that Burr was hiring soldiers for his own private army. Some said he was planning to conquer part of the Louisiana Territory and crown himself king!

Jefferson arrested Burr and brought him to trial for treason. He was found not guilty. Still, most of his old friends wanted nothing to do with him. Eventually, he had to leave America to live in Europe.

Thomas Jefferson was furious with the court's verdict. A young country had to be protected from men like Burr, who had their own personal ambitions. But the president set a good example for his countrymen, who were not always ready to follow the nation's new laws. He accepted the court's decision.

Home Again

Jefferson's second term as president ended in 1809. He returned to his hilltop home, Monticello.

His family was waiting for him. Patsy—who was called Martha now that she was grown up—had moved back home to keep house for her father. The house was full of grandchildren, relatives, and friends. Even passing strangers came to stay. It was not unusual for the Jeffersons to have several dozen guests at one time.

Thomas Jefferson was sixty-six years old now. He worried that he was getting old. But he did not have time to rest. He was always thinking of ways to improve Monticello, which had been

neglected for over twenty-five years while Jefferson served the country. He kept dreaming up new inventions, too.

One of Jefferson's inventions was a fruit picker. He attached a little basket to the end of a long pole. A hook at the end of the pole was used to pull a piece of fruit off the branch. Then the fruit fell right into the basket.

Another of Jefferson's inventions was the dumbwaiter. This was like a small elevator, hidden within the walls of the house. In many big plantation houses, the kitchen was on the floor below the dining room. Jefferson's invention eased the work of kitchen slaves, who could simply put a hot meal on the dumbwaiter in the kitchen, and then pull a rope to raise the dumbwaiter to the next floor. In the dining room, other slaves could serve the meal before it got cold.

When he was seventy-four years old, Jefferson took on yet another project. He decided to build the University of Virginia in Charlottesville, near Monticello. Jefferson designed the buildings for the new school. He raised the money and ordered the books for the library, too. He hired teachers. He even worked out the schedule of classes.

Starting the university was one of Jefferson's proudest accomplishments. When the first students arrived in 1825, he invited them to dinner at Monticello. It must have been exciting for these college students to talk about American history with the man who had written the Declaration of Independence!

Jefferson had held many important offices. But for all his success, he did not have much money. Out of office, he had many expenses. He entertained guests, improved Monticello, and took care of his family. He owed so much money that he had to sell off some of his land. He even sold his books to Congress. His beloved Monticello began to look shabby and run-down.

Even so, Jefferson had many happy moments. In 1824, when Jefferson was in his eighties, Lafayette, the Frenchman who had helped the colonies during the Revolution, came to Monticello for a visit. It had been many years since the two men had met. Jefferson came out on the porch to meet his old friend. A crowd had gathered on the lawn to watch. The two men hugged each other with tears in their eyes. The crowd cheered.

Thomas even made up with his old rival, John Adams. After so many years as enemies, the two ex-presidents began exchanging friendly letters.

The Declaration of Independence inspired people around the world to seek freedom from tyranny. Some people thought that too much freedom might hurt a young country. But they were wrong. The Declaration's demand for "life, liberty, and the pursuit of happiness" is still the most respected phrase in our history.

When the fiftieth anniversary of the Declaration of Independence was coming up, Jefferson's last wish was that he would live long enough to celebrate the great day.

On July 2, 1826, Jefferson, now eighty-three years old, took to his bed. He was very, very ill. He held on through the morning of the Fourth of July. Then, a few minutes past noon, Thomas Jefferson closed his eyes for the last time.

In Washington, the people who were celebrating Independence Day on July 4 later learned that John Adams had died that same afternoon at his house in Massachusetts. It was a startling coincidence: the second and third presidents had both been part of the committee that drafted the Declaration of Independence. Now both had died the same day, on the Declaration's fiftieth anniversary.

The generation of patriots who founded the United States of America was gone. It was time for a new era to begin.

Highlights in the Life of
THOMAS JEFFERSON

1743   Thomas Jefferson is born on April 13.

1760   Jefferson enters the College of William and Mary, where he studies to become a lawyer.

1768   Jefferson begins building Monticello. He will continue improving and remodeling the house for the rest of his life.

1772   On New Year's Day, Jefferson marries Martha Wayles Skelton.

1776   As a delegate to the Continental Congress, Jefferson is asked to write the Declaration of Independence. On July 4, his work is approved by the majority of the delegates.

1781   In May, the Revolutionary War strikes Virginia for the first time, when the British invade it. Jefferson, who is governor, flees Monticello just minutes ahead of the British soldiers.

1784   Jefferson and his daughter Patsy sail for France. For the next five years he will represent his country in Paris. His younger daughter Polly will join him later.

1789	Jefferson and his daughters return home to Virginia. In October, President George Washington officially names Jefferson secretary of state.
1790	Jefferson's daughter Martha (Patsy) marries Thomas Mann Randolph, Jr.
1797	Jefferson's political rival, John Adams, becomes the nation's second president. Jefferson is made vice-president.
1801	On March 4, Thomas Jefferson takes office as the third president of the United States.
1803	On July 4, the purchase of the Louisiana Territory from France is made public.
1804	On April 7, Jefferson's younger daughter Maria (Polly) dies at Monticello. Jefferson is reelected president.
1809	Jefferson's second term as president ends. He retires to Monticello.
1818	Jefferson founds the University of Virginia in Charlottesville.
1826	July 4 is the fiftieth anniversary of the approval of the Declaration of Independence. Thomas Jefferson dies on that day, and so does the country's second president, John Adams.